THE UNGRATEFUL TIGER

by Adam Guillain

illustrated by Anyu Rouaux

a Capstone company — publishers for children

Engage Literacy is published in the UK by Raintree.
Raintree is an imprint of Capstone Global Library Limited,
a company incorporated in England and Wales having its registered office at
264 Banbury Road, Oxford, OX2 7DY – Registered company number: 6695582

www.raintree.co.uk

Editorial credits
Marissa Kirkman and Mandy Robbins, editors; Dina Her, designer; Kelly Garvin, media
researcher; Katy LaVigne, premedia specialist

The Ungrateful Tiger
ISBN: 978 1 3982 0207 8

Printed and bound in India

CONTENTS

CHAPTER 1

WHEN THE TIGER CAME

Kim lived with his mother and father on the edge of a village. His family lived and worked on a farm.

Every day, Kim had lots of jobs to do. He would feed the chickens and take their eggs.

"Thanks for the food," the chickens would cluck.

Kim would feed the goats and then take their milk.

"Thanks for the food," the goats would bleat.

After that, Kim would take the ox out to work. Sometimes, the ox would turn the soil. Other times, the ox would carry heavy loads around the farm. The ox would pull the cart, holding much more than Kim could carry. When the work was done, Kim would feed the ox.

"Thank you for the food," the ox would snort.

Kim never thought of saying thank you to the animals. Animals had always given his family eggs and milk and a hard day's work. That's what they did.

When all his work was done, Kim would go to his favourite tree. There, he would pick some fruit from its branches and take a rest.

Life was simple. Life was safe.

Then one night, a tiger came to live in the forest nearby. No one from the village ever saw the tiger. They just saw what the tiger did.

"Help! Help!" the farm animals would call out in the dark of night. But by the time Kim and his family got there, it was always too late.

One night, the tiger took a chicken for his dinner.

The next morning, the chickens looked at Kim and clucked, "Why didn't you help us?"

Another night, the tiger took a goat.

"We called to you for help!" bleated an old goat angrily.

Kim knew the animals were upset and scared. He felt sad for them. He just didn't say or do anything to let them know.

"This tiger is causing a big problem," said Father the next day. "Fewer chickens means fewer eggs."

"And with less goat milk, there'll be less cheese," Mother added.

Father went to see the village chief. It was decided that tiger traps should be set. The villagers got to work. They dug deep, deep pits and then covered them with long, thin branches.

Kim was excited. He had never seen a tiger.

"I hope we catch it," he told Father. "I want to see what the tiger looks like."

"The best place to see a tiger is at the bottom of a pit," said Father. Kim was shocked by how serious his father's voice was. "You must remember, Kim," Father added, "to a tiger, you are food."

The very idea made Kim shiver. He felt a chill roll down his back.

CHAPTER 2

THE PROMISE

Kim was milking the old goat one morning when he heard a roar.

"The tiger!" he yelled with a shiver.

"Maaaaa!" said the old goat. "You caught him. Now you need to teach him a lesson."

Kim thought the tiger sounded scared. He ran to the edge of the pit and peered down.

The tiger's coat was the most impressive thing Kim had ever seen. Kim gazed at the orange and black striped fur.

"Let me out!" roared the huge tiger as he roamed around the bottom of the pit. "I've never done anything to hurt you."

"But you have taken a chicken and a goat from our farm," said Kim. "And killing animals is mean."

"Mean?" growled the tiger. "Digging this pit for me to fall into was mean!"

Kim thought the tiger had a point.

"And anyway," the tiger added. "I have never touched your chickens or your goats. Where is your proof?"

Kim thought about that point too. It was true, no one had ever seen the tiger do those things.

"If you don't let me out," said the tiger, "they will kill me and turn my coat into a rug."

Kim was starting to feel very sorry for the tiger. Then he remembered Father's warning. What if the tiger saw him as food?

The tiger stopped roaming and peered up.

"If you help me out, I promise I will be very, very grateful," he said. "I promise I will not do you any harm."

Kim thought the tiger looked like a king. Surely a king would keep his promise.

Just then a snake crept by.

"Are you sure you believe him?" hissed the snake.

"A promise is a promise," said Kim.

"And a tiger is a tiger," said the snake.

Kim looked around. A tree nearby had lost one of its big branches. He went to pick it up.

"Are you sure?" whispered the tree.

"A promise is a promise," said Kim.

"And a tiger is a tiger," said the tree.

Kim lifted the branch and lowered one end into the pit. In a flash, the tiger shot up the branch.

THUD!

The tiger pushed Kim down to the ground.

"Aaaaaah!" Kim gasped.

He tried to roll away and run.

But he could not move.

CHAPTER 3
THE DEAL

"I'm hungry," the tiger growled.

He glared down into Kim's scared eyes.

"Wait!" Kim begged. "You promised that if I helped you, then you would not hurt me. You promised that you would be grateful!"

"I'll give you three chances to tell me why I should not eat you," said the tiger.

The tiger liked to play with the animals he was going to eat. It was one of the things that made him feel most like a tiger.

Kim quickly called to the tree.

"Tell the tiger that he should not eat me!" he begged the tree.

Kim was sure that the tree had heard the tiger make his promise.

"Eat the boy," snapped the tree. "He takes my fruit and sits in my shade. He has never said thank you."

Kim blinked with shock. He did sit in the shade of the tree. He did eat the tree's fruit. Had he really never said thank you?

The tiger laughed and showed his claws.

"One chance over," he growled.

Kim saw his ox grazing nearby.

"Tell the tiger that he should not eat me," Kim called to the ox.

"Eat the boy," snorted the ox. "He works me hard and never says thank you."

"But I feed you and give you drinks," cried Kim.

"Never enough for all my hard work," said the ox. "Eat him!"

The tiger laughed and snapped his jaws.

"Last chance," he roared.

Kim was shaking. He quickly looked around and saw a chicken. He was about to ask the chicken for help but then he stopped.

"I take all her eggs," he thought. "She'll tell the tiger to eat me!"

Just then the old goat came along.

"Hang on," bleated the old goat.

CHAPTER 4

THE TRICK

The tiger was hungry and ready to eat up Kim. Kim looked at the old goat.

"I'm sorry I take your milk and never say thank you," he said in a hurry. "Can you please tell the tiger that he should not eat me?"

The old goat looked very thoughtful.

"Perhaps you should eat the boy," she muttered to the tiger. "But to decide for sure, I need to know all the facts."

"The facts?" asked the tiger.

"Yes," said the old goat. "Where were you exactly when he helped you?"

"I was at the bottom of that pit," said the tiger. He nodded at the pit with his head.

"That pit?" asked the old goat. She nodded to the wrong place.

"No!" growled the tiger. "That pit."

The tiger pointed at the pit with his paw.

The old goat wandered over to the pit and peered down.

"This pit?" she laughed. "This pit is too small to trap a tiger as big and powerful as you."

"No, it's not!" roared the tiger.

"Prove it," said the old goat. "I need proof."

The tiger was getting very angry.

"Proof?" he yelled. "I'll give you proof."

The tiger leaped down into the pit.

As fast as he could, Kim pulled up the branch.

"That's right," called the tiger. "I was stuck down here without that branch. Just like this. Is that enough proof?"

"It's proof that you are a fool," bleated the old goat.

"And that you are a very, very ungrateful tiger," Kim added.

Kim clapped his hands with joy, but then he stopped. The old goat was giving him a very serious and unhappy look. Kim suddenly felt a little foolish too. The tiger wasn't the only one who had been ungrateful.

"Thank you for saving my life," he said to the old goat.

"You're welcome," she said.

Kim still works on his family's farm. He still has lots of jobs to do too.

He feeds the chickens and takes their eggs.

"Thanks for the eggs," he tells them.

He feeds the goats and takes their milk.

"Thanks for the milk," he says with a smile.

After that, Kim takes the ox out to work. Sometimes he asks the ox to turn the soil. Other times, he asks the ox to carry heavy loads around the farm. When the work is done, Kim gives the ox a good long drink and lots of food.

"Thank you for all your hard work," Kim tells the ox.

"You're welcome," the animals tell him.

At the end of each day, when all his work is done, Kim goes to his favourite tree. He rests in its shade. Sometimes he picks some of its fruit.

"Thank you," Kim tells the tree.

"You're welcome," the tree replies.

But what of the ungrateful tiger? Over time, his roars became quieter and quieter. One morning, Kim went to the pit and the tiger was gone. No one knew where he went. But he was never seen again.